BÉT
√$7.25
NOV 1 '77

D1713691

a capsule course in

BLACK POETRY WRITING

a

capsule course

in

BLACK POETRY WRITING

By

Gwendolyn Brooks

Keorapetse Kgositsile

Haki R. Madhubuti

Dudley Randall

Wingate College Library

bp

Broadside Press, 12651 Old Mill Place,

Detroit, Michigan 48238

First Edition
First Printing, 1975
Second Printing, 1977
Copyright © 1975 by Gwendolyn Brooks Blakely,
Keorapetse Kgositsile, Haki R. Madhubuti,
and Dudley Randall.

Section by Gwendolyn Brooks: Reprinted by
permission of *Compton Encyclopedia Yearbook 1973.*

No part of this book can be copied, reproduced
or used in any way without written permission
from Broadside Press, 12651 Old Mill Place,
Detroit, Michigan 48238.

ISBN: 0-910296-32-4   paper $5.00

Manufactured in U.S.A.

CONTENTS

071751

INTRODUCTION

This handbook grew out of a suggestion by Gwendolyn Brooks that she compose a small textbook on writing poetry. When she generously proposed inviting other writers to participate, I was doubtful, for I feared that contradictory advice might confuse readers. However, Miss Brooks prevailed, and readers have the choice of using whatever suggestions work best with them. Some of the writers failed to meet the original deadline of December 1, 1971, but at last we have this *Capsule Course in Black Poetry Writing,* by Gwendolyn Brooks, Keorapetse Kgositsile, Haki R. Madhubuti (Don L. Lee), and Dudley Randall. Each writer's section is divided into six topics suggested by Miss Brooks.

This is not a book for the experienced writer. Only the rudiments of poetry are discussed. We do not go deeply into technique. We do, however, suggest books for further study of the technical aspects of poetry. Beginning Black poets will find here a brief background of Afro-American poetry, discussions of the role of the Black poet, guidance on self-development, and advice on writing and marketing their poetry.

The authors are all teachers and published poets. Miss Brooks is a Pulitzer Prize winner for poetry, founder of the Gwendolyn Brooks Writers Workshop, editor of their anthology *Jump Bad, A Broadside Treasury,* and publisher-editor of the annual *The Black Position.* Keorapetse Kgositsile is editor of the anthology, *The Word Is Here: Poetry from Modern Africa.* Haki R. Madhubuti is editor of Third World Press and *Black Books Bulletin,* director of the Institute of Positive Education, and author of *Dynamite Voices: Black Poets of the 1960's.* Dudley Randall is editor-publisher of Broadside Press and editor of *Broadside Series* and of the anthologies *For Malcolm, Black Poetry,* and *The Black Poets.*

Although all four authors write on the same topics, there are varying emphases. Miss Brooks sketches the background of Afro-American poetry and offers practical hints and exercises on writing. Kgositsile vents an impassioned discussion of the role and situation of the Black writer. Madhubuti presents a thoughtful explanation of an author's commitment, and guidance on the use of words, metaphors, symbols, and characters. Randall analyzes the syntactical and rhythmical structure of verse and gives suggestions on marketing. Special features are lists of books and articles for background and technique, questions asked by beginning writers with answers by Dudley Randall, and worksheets showing the growth of poems from the first jottings to the published poem.

It is impossible to make a poet. In the last analysis, the book is the man. This handbook contains, however, information and guidance from experienced published poets and editors which those who are willing to study, practice, and learn can use to increase their skills and to avoid many of the pitfalls learned the hard way by those who went before them.

> Dudley Randall
> Three Rivers, Michigan
> 5 July 1975

GWENDOLYN BROOKS

Prologue. The New Preparation. Aims. Subject Matter. Method.
The Hard Flower.

The prologue of black literature, in this country, includes the
cautious imitations of Phillis Wheatley, the burning braveries
of George Moses Horton, the wide vision of Benjamin Banneker,
the anti-slavery intonings of Frances E. W. Harper, the grand
and clarifying dramatics of Frederick Douglass, the engaging
prose reaches of William Wells Brown (first black novelist herein),
the adroit opposites of fictionist Charles W. Chesnutt, the striding
teachings of Booker T. Washington, the severe philosophical
triumphs of worldmind W. E. B. DuBois, the spicy spun sugar
of Jean Toomer, the clean sight and insight of Marcus Garvey,
black blue-printer for a new age, the Family ingatherings of
Paul Laurence Dunbar, to whom young poets of this day are
more indebted than they at first realized, the substantial sparkle
of folklorist Zora Neale Hurston, the stately scholarship *and*
limber poetics of James Weldon Johnson, the transforming
culturalism of Alain Locke, the "lyre"-mastery of Countee Cullen,
the hard and heady incense of Claude McKay, the pioneering
geniality and blackness-warmth of Langston Hughes.

And more. In general, the cry was "We are equal!"

The new black ideal italicizes black identity, black solidarity,
black self-possession and self-address. The new black literature
subscribes to these.

Furthermore, the *essential* black ideal vitally acknowledges
African roots. To those roots the new black literature coopera-
tively subscribes.

The prevailing understanding: black literature is literature
BY blacks, ABOUT blacks, directed TO blacks. ESSENTIAL
black literature is the distillation of black life. Black life is
different from white life. Different in nuance, different in "nitty
gritty." Different *from* birth. Different *at* death.

There is frequent impatience with the phrase "black literature."
"Can literature be black? Can literature be white? Is not literature
just literature?"

1966. 1967. 1968. Years of explosion. In those years a young
black with pen in hand responded not to pretty sunsets and

3

the lapping of lake water but to the speech of physical riot and spiritual rebellion. Young blacks went to see "The Battle of Algiers" rather than the latest Rock Hudson movie. Young blacks stopped saluting Shakespeare, A. E. Housman, T. S. Eliot. They began to shake hands with Frantz Fanon, Malcolm X— gulping down the now "classic" *The Wretched of the Earth,* the *Autobiography* and *Message to the Grass Roots.* And after such seeing, after such gulping, there *had* to be a Difference. There had to be hard reckonings. There had to be an understanding that NOW the address must be to blacks; that shrieking into the steady and organized deafness of the white ear was frivolous—perilously innocent; was "no 'count." There were things to be said to black brothers and sisters and these things—annunciatory, curative, inspiriting—were to be said forthwith, without frill, and without fear of the white presence. The initial trend was away from decoration, away from dalliance. There was impatience with idle embroidery, with what was considered avoidance, avoidance of the gut issue, the blood fact. Literary rhythms altered! Sometimes the literature seemed to issue from pens dipped in, *stabbed* in, writhing blood. Music was very important. It influenced the new pens. There were veerings from Glenn Miller and Benny Goodman to Coltrane, Ornette Coleman, Charlie Mingus, Charles Earland—from "I'll Be Seeing You" to "Soulful Strut."

Black Fire, a fat anthology of "the new writing," was issued by Larry Neal and Imamu Amiri Baraka, then LeRoi Jones, in 1968. Pandemonium. Whites attacked this "racist" volume. The young blacks, richly ready for this compilation of black love, rage, program design and resolution, coldly shook off the term "racist," and carried above them, like a banner, their own endorsement of Stokely Carmichael's definition: "You are a racist *only* if you oppress other racial groups." *Black Fire* was an electric springboard. Flaming poetry, fiction, drama, essays. Especially did the essays "make a difference." They were listened to, loved, quoted. "The West is dying, as it must, as it should," shouted Lary Neal. . . . "the black artist must link his work to the struggle for his liberation and the liberation of his brothers and sisters." Herein, Larry Neal wanted black literature to aim at collective ritual—"but ritual directed at the destruction of useless, dead ideas. . . . black literature must become an integral part of the community life style. . . . We can learn more about what [black] poetry is by listening to the cadences in Malcolm's speeches than from most of Western poetics." James T. Stewart, essayist, painter, and singer, opened the book with his essay, "The Development of the Black Revolutionary Artist": "We must be estranged from the dominant culture. This estrangement must be nurtured in order to generate and energize our black artists." James T. Stewart is disdainful of the concept of fixity. He advises disregard for "perpetuation of the product—the picture, the statue, the temple." (And certainly the piece of "literature!")

The new feeling, among the *earnest* new young black creators, was that concern for long-lastingness was western and was wrong. One created a piece of art for the enrichment, the instruction, the extension of one's people. Its usefulness may or may not be exhausted in a day, a week, a month, a year. There was no prayerful compulsion—*among the earnest*—for its idle survival into the centuries. The word went down: we must chase out Western measures, rules, models.

In "Not Just Whistling Dixie" A. B. Spellman, poet, professor and jazz authority, contributed a particular item of significance, relevant to black literature as easily as it is relevant to black music: "It was Charlie Parker's revolutionary approach to self, society and existence that illuminates those brillant arpeggios and lays the basis of his genius."

And after such turning, nothing could be the same. . . .

II

Much of the work that preceded the days of considerable black fire belongs in a category I call "condition literature." You remember, in "Song of Myself," Walt Whitman loves animals because they do not tirelessly "whine about their condition." A good many of us who preceded the pioneering influence of Baraka did a lot of poetic, dramatic, and fictional whining. And a lot of that lot was addressed to white people. We sensed ourselves crying "UP" to them. "Help us," we seemed to cry. We were fascinated by the sickness of the black condition. One of my own twenty year old poems semi-begs: "Grant me that I am human, that I hurt, that I can cry."

1966. 1967. 1968. The younger people pooh-poohed or cursed this attitude. Insofar as they could, they shelved whites. (In Chicago, Carolyn Rodgers, indeed, never "went downtown," would not "shop in the Loop"). They shelved what some of them called The White Thang. They favored a Black Thang.

The Harlem Renaissance writers and the post-Harlem renais-
sance writers did not create in terms of a Black Thang. They
created, and felt, in terms of integration. The great "Negro"
dream was "Hand in hand toge-ether!" Langston Hughes, who
identified himself as the "darker brother," wanted to sit at "the
table" and wanted "them" to "see how beautiful" he was. "Tired"
Fenton Johnson decided that it is "better to die, than to grow
up and find that you are colored," but this was *because* he,
as "darker brother," could not get a grip on the great American
goodies. Claude McKay's "If We Must Die" was remarkably in
the spirit of the late sixties but mid-fury he weakened, evincing
a regrettable concern for and interest in "the monsters we defy."
"Though dead" (that's for sure, the poet acknowledges: you know
how strong they are, how powerful; black victory of *any* kind
or size is not to be thought of—this is THE MAN) we'll be
gratifyingly *honored* (how beautiful) . . .

> even the monsters we defy
> Shall be constrained to honor us though dead!

Langston Hughes, however, in many of his poems was able
to put his keen ear to the latter Black ground, was able to
hear the "militant" rumblings therein, was able to interpret
correctly a portion of the latter significance:

> I could tell you
> if I want to
> what makes me
> what I am.
> But I really
> don't want to
> and you don't
> give a damn.

Baraka, feeling much the same, could "bring it all on down"
into the succinct, no-nonsense incandescence of "SOS."
Richard Wright made us look at helpless black men—whose
histories were fear-flight-fate, in varying parts. But even though
he could speak meaningfully to blacks about what blacks know
and instantly recognize, he hoped to attract, stun, charm and
enlist white sympathy, to stimulate white empathy.
Ralph Ellison. Says the important critic George Kent of Ralph

Ellison: "Permeating all his statements is the emphasis which he gives to the Americanness of all positions and his engagement with all strands of the American cultural fabric."

James Baldwin was finally driven to a dire promise. "The *Fire* Next Time!" It was a launch. But it hurt him. There was pain. He had made such a heavy investment in integration.

Then came Baraka, rejecting all lovely little villanelles and sonnets—to Orpheus or anything else. Prettiness was out. Fight-fact was in. Baraka demanded black poems. Poems must be teeth, fists, daggers, guns, cop-wrestlers. Why? These would be cleansers! "Clean out the world for virtue and love," Baraka ordered.

Came Don L. Lee, a further pioneer. Born in 1942, on February twenty third, the birthday of DuBois, he told us "The black artist by defining and legitimizing his own reality becomes a positive force in the black community." He told us "Black poetry is like a razor; it's sharp and will cut deep." He believed in speaking directly to his people. He addressed them in shrewd, tough words whose meaning they could not mistake. They could not mistake, either, the attendant affection, affection for all blackness. Long ago I saw him as a screamer in the sun. And David Llorens accurately wrote of him "At once he will be hailed and damned for the same reason: because he refuses to write a single line in forgetfulness of his blackness." Don L. Lee was the stimulus and drive for an entire *new* "renaissance" of fire-filled young black poets who were given a platform by older poet Dudley Randall (who is Broadside Press of Detroit). Etheridge Knight. John Raven. Sonia Sanchez. Nikki Giovanni. Everett Hoagland. James Emanuel. Doughtry Long. Ronda Davis. Walter Bradford. Mike Cook. James Cunningham. Others. (Don Lee himself soon started his Third World Press in Chicago, and published the work of Carolyn Rodgers, Johari Amini, Sterling Plumpp, Imanu Baraka, Hoyt Fuller, George Kent, Keorapetse Kgositsile, Dudley Randall. . . .)

A rich prose-poetry piece in the new mood is the slain George Jackson's "Soledad Brother." Jagged-poignant and merciless, as are many black prison writings throughout the United States in this day.

Contemporary talents in the field of fiction include Toni Cade Bambara—*Gorilla, My Love;* John O. Killens who wrote *And Then We Heard the Thunder, Youngblood, Cotillion,* and who is also an essayist and scriptwriter; Julian Mayfield, *The Long*

Night and *The Grand Parade;* Ossie Davis, *Purlie Victorious;*
Ishmael Reed, celebrated especially for his "tour de force" *Yellow
Back Radio Broke Down;* Sam Greenlee, *The Spook Who Sat
By the Door;* Ann Petry, *The Street.* In the field of drama, eminent,
of course, is Baraka whose *Dutchman, Toilet,* and *Slave* were
style-setters: but we have also the impact of such innovators
as penetrating Ed Bullins, *A Son, Come Home, Goin' a Buffalo,
In the Wine Time;* and Douglas Turner Ward, *Day of Absence*
and *Happy Ending;* Lonne Elder, *Ceremonies in Dark Old Men;*
Adrienne Kennedy, *A Rat's Mass;* Ron Milner, *Who's Got His
Own* and *The Warning: A Theme for Linda;* Charles Gordone,
the recent Pulitzer Prizewinner, *No Place To Be Somebody.*

Further, there are black critics for the curative assessment
of black literature. Thoughtful blacks understand that white
critics, even those with the best will in the world, even those
with the strictest "objectivity," even those with commendable
warmth, even the most brilliant and widely-read, cannot judge
black works with the nuanceful intuition and empathy of blacks
intimate with both substance and essence of the life involved.
In addition to longtime-valued J. Saunders Redding, some of
the strongest of these contemporary black literary critics are
George Kent, (*Blackness and the Adventure of Western Culture*);
Addison Gayle, (*The Black Situation* and *Claude McKay* and
editor of such anthologies as *The Black Aesthetic*); Hoyt Fuller,
(editor of *Black World,* and author of *Journey to Africa*); Clayton
Riley, *Liberator* reviewer; Haki Madhubuti (Don Lee), *Dynamite
Voices;* Stanley Crouch and Ron Welburn, poet-essayists; Joe
Goncalves; Paula Giddings; Francis Ward; Lisbeth Gant; Houston
Baker; Eugenia Collier; Carolyn Gerald. These people are wel-
come in the pages of such new-purpose magazines as *Journal
of Black Poetry* (Joe Goncalves edits this), *Black World, The
Black Scholar, Black Books Bulletin, Essence, Freedomways,
Nommo, Free Lance, The Black Position.* (A serious magazine
of an older stamp is *Phylon,* in which the respected critic Arthur
P. Davis has written since the forties.)

There are additional black publishing companies, too. Chicago's
Johnson Publishing Company (all of historian Lerone Bennett's
work is published by John H. Johnson's press), New York's
Emerson Hall Publishers and Third Press; Newark's Jihad
Productions, directed by Baraka. These companies work sympa-
thetically with the new writers, knowing when to *allow extrava-
gantly* and when to *pull in the reins.* They are not concerned

that white critics, referring inevitably to European "standards," spit on the fledglings.

The understood black station now is an organic "Enough!", a creative rebellion that often yearns toward revolution. There is certainly no going back to puny implorings, to integration-worship, to labeled slavery.

Black literature: a reflection of the black mood, intuition, fury and resolve.

Where is it going?

There may be more of the oblique subtleties of Ishmael Reed—with extensions, and departures. There may be further Larry Neal blendings of music, ritual and black homily—with extensions, and departures. There may be more of the *seasoned folk* delineations of Lucille Clifton. There will be black lyrics, reliant on the specifics of black dailyness for their inspiration. Here is Cheryl Davis' bitter-sweet and educated comprehension of special rejection: rejection of blacks by blacks—because of blackness:

> like most children
> I was born
> on the day
> my mother
> couldn't stand it
> any longer.
>
> And from all over
> people came to see
> what she had had;
> not knowing of course
> that she had had *me.*
>
> When they found
> that she had had *me*
> they all left,
> wondering
> how she could ever
> have done
> such a thing.

There will be differences. Differences only the new developers—or the advanced old—can apprehend. But the differences will be in form and approach.

For certainly a present basic which I recently observed will continue: an agreeable invasion of the folk, an appropriation of supplies, wonderful supplies, only to shape, to fill, to enhance with substantial embroidery a fundamental strength, which is then returned with proud respect.

A Few Hints toward the Making of Poetry:

1. Language—ordinary speech. Today we do not say "Thou saintly skies of empyrean blue through which there soarest sweetest bird of love." Forget ecstasy, ethereal, empyrean, wouldst, canst. Do not use 'neath, e'er, ne'er, 'mid, etc.

2. If you allude to a star, say precisely what that star means to *you*. If you feature a garden, speak of that garden *most personally*. If you have murdered in a garden, the grass and flowers (and weeds) will mean something different to you than to someone who has only planted or picked.

3. Try telling the reader a little less. He'll, she'll love you more, and will love your poem more, if you allow him to do a little digging. Not *too* much, but *some*.

4. Avoid cliches.

> gentle flowers
> sad lament
> deepest passion
> the wind howled

Occasionally a cliche can be redeemed:

> the gentle flowers shrieked and killed the sun.
> the sad lament was lovely, and I laughed.

For here the pictures and concepts are so outrageous that the cliche is elevated into a contribution.

Here is a cliche-stanza composed by me for your redemption. Redeem each line:

> Sweet sun, wouldst thou but shine o'er all
> With thine ethereal ecstasy,
> And chase dark clouds from out mine soul
> For all thy fair eternity.

5. In a poem (and *I* believe in any piece of writing) every word must *work*. Every word, and indeed every comma, every semi-colon (if such are used—they needn't be). Every dash (and poets should use few dashes: they are usually indeterminate, weak) has a job to do and must be about it. Not one word or piece of punctuation should be used which does not strengthen the poem.

6. Loosen your rhythm so that it sounds like human talk. Human talk is not exact, is not precise. Sometimes human talk "has flowers," but if it "has flowers," those flowers (as I have said in my poem "Young Africans") "must come out to the road."

7. You must make your reader believe that what you say *could* be true. Think of your efforts to be convincing *and* entertaining when you are gossiping. You use gesture, touch, tone-variation, facial expression. Try persuading your wordage—SOMEHOW!—to do all the things your body does when forwarding a piece of gossip.

8. Remember that ART is refining and evocative translation of the materials of the world!

KEORAPETSE KGOSITSILE

Prologue

> . . . Say you float above
> the dollar-green eye of the hustler whose
> purpose is cloaked in dashikis and glib
> statements about revolution.
>
> Say you float
> untouchably above this menace, does
> your purpose, if there be one, propose
> to be less impotent than this poem?

So where does my poetry come from? I wrote, first of all, because I enjoyed writing. I also considered the writing relevant to our goals, that is, instrumental in taking me closer to taking up arms against the oppressor after my consciousness had brought me to a more concrete level of creativity, collective social action, the only gateway to our liberation. See, I've tried to listen attentively to demystified people who know very precisely where we are, and what we can do about it if we don't like it.

When you make a statement, comment or observation, you create and define relationships. You assert, propose or oppose certain values through the words you use. This is tied up with traditions, patterns of thinking, aesthetic considerations, myths, social realities, histories, which the writer must know and try to *understand* in order to sharpen and strengthen his or her voice.

But what if a people's spirit has been gangrened to impotence through perversions like slavery, distortion of values, myopic vision and so forth? When we have been programmed into harmless freaks in institutions of European design?

So now to be fully aware, once again, and with more clarity, of our powerlessness, our impotence . . . Really, what relevance, or use, could poems have? To entertain us in our impotence?

And some will call the new literature by black writers *revolutionary.* How can you have a revolutionary literature without a revolution to form and inform, to shape and strengthen the writer's sensibility?

We must be honest though the *truth,* or the stench of our lives, be painful. We can be precise. Though we are connected to all time, we belong, unarguably, to our time. If you are in filth, your looking up at the skies or imagining yourself as a bird flying way up there will not clean up what needs to be cleaned nor will it move you away from it. If there is any validity to the making of a black poetry, as in the making of any other attempts in any other areas of our lives, that poetry has to explore and report exactly where we are. And there is nothing revolutionary about where we are, which is who we are, which is what we do as a people. Where we are is a filthy, ugly place of predominantly European design. Fanon and Malcolm died advising us to move from here. Ayi Kwei Armah and Ouologuem, among our novelists, have shown us, in images heavy with the stench, the ugliness of where we are. Also, but with a handling almost bordering on sympathy, Achebe and Ngugi. But our poetry, with a few exceptions, avoids this ugliness, which becomes, finally, itself ugly and mystifying. The only portion of our poets that consistently seeks to express a part of where we are with admirable skill, seriousness and depth of feeling wrung from the collective reservoir, is the musicians. And I haven't heard the toughest of the musicians label themselves revolutionary. Say B. B. King runs into a young blood who is trying to play European music and the blood is moved to a point where he wants to learn some things from B. B. Say finally he learns how to play the blues, could we say any more than that B. B. King taught the brother how to express his feelings and experience as a black musician? Is it revolutionary to be authentic and articulate?

We need exposé-poems, the stench leaping off the page leaving no room for us to hide in closets where we whore with Europe but come out on the marketplaces proclaiming our authentic black virginity.

We need to stop idealizing and idolizing the brother on the block. He is no hero. He is a casualty, a victim. And he will remain a pawn, like all of us, until we *live* together, until we all work together to rebuild our family. And if poetry is creative activity steeped in reality, which it must be in order to be valid, we need poems that report on and explore the tragedy of our time. The coldness of the European independence farce in Nigeria taught J. P. Clark to think of *Casualties.* Okigbo left us *Path of Thunder.* And there is Jean Toomer's *Cane* and Gwen Brooks' *In The Mecca.*

Wingate College Library

The New Preparation

There are standards of excellence in the making of poetry, as in the making of anything else. However, any worship of literary craftsmanship divorced from the realities of the time a writer lives in is a perversion; it is arty corniness as distinct from any authentic attempt at artistic expression. Because any authentic artistic expression is unarguably social; it is very exact about where its maker is or wants to be. Roots it is we are talking about. All cultural explorers, and the writer is certainly one, start off from specific roots which color their vision and define the allegiances of the work of art they produce. Many writers' conferences, or carnivals, I have been to; a lot of garbage that passes for black writing; a lot of 'cultural' nationalism rhetoric and so on, are all finally as bankrupt, as impotent, as the latest handshake. So I turn to other sources to prepare myself to write. My earliest memories and I read and reread Malcolm, Fanon, a few novelists, some history and listen to a lot of music in an attempt to understand precisely where we are without any illusions. Most poets I read for entertainment or to study our vulgar contradictions.

Since the Word is at its most expressive in poetry, part of my preparation to make a few poems is studying words, their meanings, the ones the dictionaries don't talk about, their subtle implications which either nourish, damage or destroy people's minds. Take, for instance, words like non-white, Afro-American or African-American. Can one be African and American (European) at the same time without being emotionally and mentally crippled? So that, to me, unless when we say Afro- or African-American we are being descriptive of where some Africans have been forced to travel and slave for European fun and profit, the terms become highly questionable. We even say *bright* or *brilliant* when we mean *intelligent. Fair* when we mean *just. Enlighten* when we mean *educate;* and think nothing of the European racism of our statements. In South Africa we even went so far as to say *jewish* or *kosher* for *good!* and thought we were so cool.

Aims

>Words, be they elegant
>As verse or song

Robust and piercing as sunshine
Or hideous memories of our
Cowardice in bondage are meaningless unless
They be the solid coil around our desire and method
Or the "most competent rememberer."

About five or six years ago Lindsay Barrett, with frustrations, desires and preoccupations similar to mine, asked me how one could explain the mad desire and determination to keep looking at a sore with a magnifying glass. I had ready answers then. I had enormous strength supported by my intense hatred of whatever European tendencies we had and the belief that all the worthlessness was going up in flames. My poetry of that period sizzles with those flames:

> . . . Self-born
> Maumau splits time's skull
> With spearpoint flesh of mystic mask
> Of built-in SHOTGUN weaved
> In sounds like my daughter's
> Memory of anguished joy in nigger-
> Hard shadows screwing
> The right moment . . .

I have no ready answers now. My aims? When I write every line I write will contain particles of poison for the oppressor; every line will either be an element of entertainment for us or it will be part of an attempt at commenting on or exploring where we are today, bringing out the uglinesses of this place and time in such a precise manner that, hopefully, I will be adding something of use to the forces among us who try to persuade us through what they do to be people, to live again. Again we are talking about land and power. After reclaiming the land on which to create, and to consolidate whatever resources of power to protect and inspire us, only then can we talk of a spirituality that links and binds us together; a serenity brought about by a sense of purpose and meaning in our lives, evidenced in the way we live past any saying of it; Brotherhood and Unity being then the way we live and not a mere game run on the people by some glib, money-bound parasite.

Also *continuity*, not *return*. The African elite, the assimilationists, highly unproductive even in the area of ideas, talk

of a return to African ways. So do the titular Cultural National-
ists. Remember Fanon warned us that this blind idealism is
finally reactionary? But the people with some amount of clarity
know that our ways still exist among the majority of the people;
in most cases covered up or twisted around in a hostile white
environment, but still there. They can be unveiled and unleashed.
The differences between Kunene, who is about continuity, and
Senghor, who talks of a return and a "civilizing of the univer-
sal,"—whatever that is—should illustrate what I'm talking
about. My sense of aesthetics is tied up to, and with, this
continuity. If a poem I write is ritualistic and inspired enough
its content—African worldview (philosophical orientation) and
my view of the world (my thinking and understanding)—plus
its music or sound patterns reflect my connectedness to the
collective circle without sacrificing the realities of the present,
the cycle or time I live in as in *For Ipeleng:*

First I isolate a specific occurrence in my time, the birth of
my daughter:

> I saw her come here with no words,
> arms flailing air, past mother, thigh
> and blood. . . .

This, especially the image of blood, leads to a comment about
origins, an assertion of the life principle, destruction/creation:

> and blood. Here we begin again

It is the blood that flows during a specific birth which is a
concrete manifestation of natural process, ritual of origin and
continuity, tension at the meeting point of pain and joy, twin
source of any affirmation of the life principle, destruc-
tion/creation. My mother might say it is those things in life
that matter which will give you pain as you learn to understand
life. "She knew now that marriage did not make love. *Janie's
first dream was dead, so she became a woman.*" (Italics mine).
Zora Neale Hurston says of Janie in *Their Eyes Were Watching
God.* Death of principle, failure of some god, as Wilson Harris
might say. And Chairman Mao has taught us about contra-
dictions. In Yoruba culture Ogun is the god of war and creativity.

Okay, back to Ipeleng in her new environment which she seems to be already absorbing, perhaps with intuition, collective memory:

> We shall know each other
> by the root of our appetite
> or rhythm; Big Mama Juicy
> Aneb seemed to say.
> Her eye direct as comment. As
> roaches or rats. As heads cracked
> open for fun or law & order
> in this strange place

in spite of which the affirmation of the life principle I spoke of at the beginning of the poem forces open the doors to my dreams, my hopes against the uglinesses of the realities of this time and place:

> When I woke up one morning
> I saw her coming in the stillness
> of her day and want. My eye sprung out
> to embrace a season of dreams.

but not for long. The present is here, it is immediate, it knows no peace:

> But she asked: if mother or father
> is more than parent, is this my land
> or merely soil to cover my bones?

Subject Matter

> So was I born again stubborn and fierce
> screaming in a slum.
> It was a city and a coffin space for home
> a river running, prisons, hospitals
> men drunk and dying, judges full of scorn
> priests and parsons fooling gods with words
> and me, like a dog tangled in rags
> spotted with sores powdered with dust
> screaming with hunger, angry with life and men.
> —Martin Carter

And my subject matter, it should be clear by now, is us in our time; the complexities of our inner landscapes and our outer realities.

Love and Friendship:

>Morning smiles
>In your eye
>Like a coy moment
>Captured by an eternal
>Noon . . .

Our Dreams:

>In the stillnesses of the night
>Informed by the rhythm of your spirit
>We hear the song of warriors
>And rejoice to find fire in our hands
>"Aint no mountain high enough . . ." Dig it,
>The silences of the wind know it too
>"Aint no valley low enough . . ."
>Freedom, how do you do!

Their Quick Destruction by the Invasion of Reality:

>What you know is merely a point
>of departure. So let's move. But we have
>been dead so long and *continue*. There will
>be no songs this year. We no longer
>sing. Except perhaps some hideous
>gibberish like james brown making believe
>he is american or beautiful or proud. Or
>some fool's reference to allah who, like
>jehovah, never gave a two-bit shit about niggers.

Our Endurance:

>But the melody of memory
>Lingered strained by bloodstained
>Diamond, whiplash
>And mother turned shadow

Our Potential:

> Go on, brother, say it. Talk
> the talk slaves are afraid to live
>
> "What does a penny buy?"
> When Brown is Black

Affirmation of the Life Principle:

> All things come to pass
> When they do, if they do
> All things come to their end
> When they do, as they do
> So will the day of the stench of oppression
> Leaving nothing but the lingering
> Taste of particles of hatred
> Woven around the tropical sun

Identity:

> I know my name
> which denies no mask
> made obsolete by ghouls
> and oxfords pants
> that covered no balls. . . .
> and I know my name
> celebrating all time love hate
> measured in broken chains

and much more. Whatever I am moved to isolate and celebrate and/or comment on. But wherever I might start from the poetic statement I make is, as it always should and will be, unequivocally and unapologetically social.

Method

Vision. The way I think and feel every day. So when I make a poem I don't have to think. I record the images as they flow or tumble out of my insides the best way I can.

I hate aggressors. I wouldn't bully a poem any more than I would bully another man, woman or child. Given my frame of reference, my values—and here the aesthetic is inseparable from the social—I let a poem come when it will come and let it demand its standards. Its allegiances, its social and emotional placement.

The Hard Flower

Authenticity. Relevance. Directness. Specificity. I suppose now that I write not because I still enjoy doing it but because I don't really know how to do anything else, I am much more critical of my work than, perhaps, I have ever been before. I am equally critical of other people's work, especially my contemporaries. So after making a poem, I check it to see if it carries my worldview, which is collective; and my view of the world, which is a result of my understanding and ordering of our outer realities and my internal landscape; I check to see if it has any relevance to our lives, even if it be no more than entertainment, without corniness. If it passes the test without my bullying it into anything I keep it, read it or show it to a number of friends before I publish it. If it fails the test it goes where all other garbage goes.

For a number of years I used to try out everything I wrote on Melba as soon as I would finish writing it. Not any more. A wife is a wife and a workshop is a workshop although they are not necessarily mutually exclusive.

HAKI R. MADHUBUTI
(DON L. LEE)

Prologue:

Writers write. What they write about tells the reader to what extent they are involved with the real world.

Writing for me is a difficult process. I write best under pressure, under a deadline set for me by someone or one that I set for myself. I am not a *professional* or a *leisure* writer. What I mean is I do not earn my livelihood from writing nor do I allot special time in the day just to write. Much of my writing is note taking. I take an abundance of notes and these notes, at a later time, are developed into poems, essays and occasional fiction. Writing for me is also a form of life-therapy but *it is not my life.* My life is too complex to be limited to one stimulus. For me this is good and has worked.

Writers should be questioners of the world and doers within the world. Question everything. And don't be satisfied with the quick surface answers. Richard Wright was a questioner. We can see it in his works, the fiction and nonfiction. W. E. B. DuBois was a questioner—his output tripled that of the "average" writer while maintaining a high level of quality and content. Both men were of the world but, in their own way, refused to be subordinated to the world. They were fighters, always aware of the war and writing was a war weapon. And writing at its best for them was a tool, a vocation, a hammer to be used for the survival and development of the Race.

The writers who endure are not necessarily the best. Yet, most do have something to say and say it in a way that people can understand and relate to. Langston Hughes's work is an excellent example of style and content that Black people relate to. His jazz poetry and Simple folk tales not only established him as a "professional" writer of the very best order but earned him the title "Dean" of Black writers from his own people. Sterling Brown also comes to mind in terms of original style and content, his poetry and essays exemplify the highest tradition of Black oral communication combined with scholarly research. For me, the content as well as good writing is important. Beautiful writing that does not say anything is just and only *that,* beautiful writing. Yet, bad writing containing the most revolutionary ideas is equally, first and last, *bad writing.* A standard must be met if the writer is to communicate effectively. The ability to develop a style that is clear, original and communicative is what separates writers from non-writers.

Originality must be stressed. All too often the young writer will unconsciously copy the elder and not allow room for the development of a personal inner voice. Sometimes in our efforts to be original we *over-write.* We try to be too "intelligent," too wordy, too on top of things. In over-writing we use language and metaphors that usually are of another culture and another time. This is not originality.

In many ways all writers are re-creators. We take in the world and retell it, reinterpret it for others in a form and style that should be unique for the writer, the readers and our times. Our times are space age times and words come and go like Chicago's weather. The way the writer uses the words tells us as much about him or her as a word-user than anything else. The major distinction that can be made between writers (other than forms they work in) is their ability to say the same thing differently, originally using and "mis-using" the language at will. The language is the tool, the weapon, and they must train themselves to use it as a carpenter trains with wood and nails, or as a farmer trains with the earth.

Aims

The writer is the lively but lonely investigator, the seeker of unknowns, the wanderer through back alleys, power corridors and into the far reaches of his own mind and that of his people. Essentially the loneliness comes from the demands of the writing form; generally, although there are exceptions, one does not write as a group. Writing is a personal occupation, one man/woman, one pen or typewriter. Once you leave the research, the study, to do battle with the blank sheet of paper, you are on your own. Writing is a lonely vocation that is bound to affect the writers and those closest to them. When the writer begins to work the most important concern is the relationship between the writer and his subject. The central question becomes: How to bring life to the given subject?

This above all else requires discipline. The creative process is a discipline process which most writers have had to teach themselves. In most cases as soon as the writing begins the interruptions seem to multiply—these interruptions are real and unreal. Each phone call is attacked or ignored because the writer is more, or less, sensitive to the uses of his or her time. Family relationships are altered during this period. Also, the book that could have been read easily two months ago becomes a *priority* now!—not because the book is essential to the writer's subject but because it becomes a part of the writer's internal interruptions. These types of interference are often rationalized as direct contributions to the writing. Nonsense. Writers waste time, as do most people, this is why discipline is so important.

Originality

Originality for the Black poet essentially means you must either have something new and insightful to say (important, with depth) or you must find a new way of saying something that has already been said. The way in which you say something is referred to as "style." The originality we are concerned with here is what you have to say. Such themes as the *fact* that Europeans are bent on destroying African peoples, that the black middle class often copies the styles and values of Europeans and that African peoples need to get together are not original. This does not mean they are not important or true. The three themes stated above have been realities of our lives for a very long time now, and hundreds of poems on those themes have not altered that reality. Thus, if you choose to deal with such themes (and they must be dealt with), you *must* create a form/style which is original, which is not a copy of other poets. Conrad Kent Rivers once wrote:

> A black poet must bear in mind
>   the misery.
> The color-seekers fear poems
>   they can't buy for a ten-dollar
> bill or with a clever contract.
>   Some black kid is bound to read you.

The following poem by Sister Sharon Scott which appeared in the September issue of *Black World,* 1971, illustrates one aspect of what we mean by originality.

and so,
i have decided
to
consider it
a
special time
because of a
particular
opening
and,

to let it be as such
and
all that comes to me
or that
i can catch
is special
is extradordinary
and,

if it all shall leave us or
the world should end or
whatever ending force

i can hold—
whatever we have,
we have anyway
whatever is coming
it comes because
we have brought it here.

take upon yourself,
yourselves
and your needs.

remember the delicacies
remember the time.

might come
more than likely
we will go but
NOW
    i work and
week myselves
into a plan

and let nothing
short
of the air i cling to
distort my efforts
or their comings.

i will
take with me
what is ready to come
what is ready to go
without my having to pull
it any longer that

Lack of Imagery, Color, Metaphor, Detail, Character:

There are many ways to make a poem "a memorable experience," Gwendolyn Brooks says. One can use images, that is pictures, visible pictures, which carry the characteristics of your subject or which suggest the meaning and mood you are trying to create. One of the strengths of using images and metaphors is that often they carry the weight of symbols, that is they suggest multiple levels of meaning to your reader as well as allow him to read his own experience into the image or metaphor. Another important technique for making the poem a "memorable experience" is to create characters, real people with whom the reader can feel and empathize. In poetry, however, when creating characters, the poet should search for only those crucial characteristics of that human being which symbolize what he is most essentially about. Images, metaphors, characters take on visibility, become memorable by the use of concrete details. The following are examples of what we mean.

1) ". . . Prophet Williams, young beyond St. Julia,/and rich with Bible; pimples, pout: who reeks/with lust for his disciple, is an engine/of candid steel hugging combustibles.

Gwendolyn Brooks created this character in the poem "In The Mecca." She is able to establish through suggestion the real character of Prophet Williams. She does this in part through concrete choice of metaphor. When she compares the prophet's passion (for his disciples) to an "engine of candid steel hugging combustibles," she is able to suggest on the one hand the great power, probably physical power, of the prophet and on the other the coldness and real dispassion or lack of passion of the prophet.

In this case, then, the metaphor allows her to make several statements at the same time, using very few words (simple words).

2) In the long poem "In the Mecca" we can see how Sister Brooks chooses those select concrete details which are crucial to an intimate understanding of that character. She says of Briggs, a young brother intimate with the neighborhood gang,

> Briggs is adult as a stone

The stone as an image or metaphor for Briggs' development is most appropriate as it allows her to make several profound statements with only six simple words. A stone is hard as Briggs is hard. A stone does not grow as organic matter like human beings grow, thus suggesting Briggs has reached a point beyond which he cannot go. It also suggests a certain one-dimensional aspect of Briggs' character.

3) For a sensitive use of color, details and concrete images we can turn to Everett Hoagland in his first book "Black Velvet." In the first stanza of "Love Child: A Black Aesthetic" he writes:

> sweet baked apple dappled cinnamon speckled sin of mine
> nutmeg freckled peach brandy and amber wine woman
>   WOW
> with your piping hot and finger popping black african
> pepper pot not stopping steaming coffee flowing creaming
> the brown sugar growing cane candy coming cocoa going
> crazy 'bout brown sugar teases GOOD GOD and pleases
>   SWEET
> JESUS that honey stained soul trained slow molasses ass
> and GODDAM candied yam and sweet potato pie
> thighs and sweet raisin tipped coconut tits raising cane
>   sugar
> stone brown sugar bowl belly to the bone to the bone

Triteness:

Often the beginning writer starts learning his craft by imitating others. In the beginning stages of writing, this may be necessary. We do advise brothers and sisters, however, that when you've only been writing a year or so, you probably haven't developed your craft to the point where you'd want it published. At this point, it is probably better to try to get published individual poems in magazines or your local black newspapers. Dudley Randall, editor of Broadside Press in Detroit, tells a story of Robert Hayden and his zeal to be published early. Some of these very early poems—now out of print—Brother Randall confides, Brother Hayden doesn't want seen today.

The problem of triteness—that of using words and phrases which have been used over and over again and are no longer fresh and vivid—we have found usually falls into the category of the street rap or in the form of imitating 19th century european phrases (personifying the sun and moon, "thou," etc.) The problem with the rap is that it is a potentially very powerful form. To exert its power, the brother who uses it must do more than copy or imitate the vocabulary of the rap. The brother who chooses this form must create an originality and a tension on the printed page; using the words of the rap alone on a piece of paper cannot of itself carry the nuance and rhythm of a brother on the corner rapping out his mouth. In the same way, for example, Langston Hughes in his blues poems—because he only "copied" the superficial form of the blues lyric—could not really reach the power of a Blind Lemon or a Muddy Waters. The printed page imposes limitations that sound does not.

Examples of current phrases which reflect the content/concern of much of the contemporary black poetry, but which in the last few years have become trite are—

Warrior	soul
ebony	universe
black	cosmos
whitey	nigger
Queen of the Nile	genocide
rite on/right on	vibrations
African warrior	black is beautiful
pig	revolution
pride	respect
	change

Haphazard Choice of Words

The problem of haphazard choice of words generally falls into the following categories:

1) TOO MANY WORDS—Sometimes the beginning poet will use complete grammatical sentences (using connectives like

"and," etc.). Often just an elliptical phrase will do. It is just as important for the poet to know what to take out as to know what to put in. The following example from Sister Johari Amini (Let's Go Some Where) shows how effective the use of only those words (carefully chosen) necessary to create the intense moment of message and mood can be:

> I am too past youth
> too strong
> too black
> to cry
>   still . . .
> need
> comes: a steadied
> profuseness: insensitive
> spreading
> spreading

In this example, the use of single words as full lines draws attention to each word.

2) WORDS VAGUE AND ABSTRACT—The raw material of the poet—the word and sounds. Gwen Brooks has said that a poem should be a "memorable experience." The right, most appropriate, most *exact* choice of words is part of what makes the *experience* of the poem memorable. The following examples from Sister Brooks illustrate how the right word is specific and concrete in nature, yet often carries the massive power of the symbol (allowing each reader to be consciously directed into a myriad of experiences, emotions and meaning). We see also from Sister Brooks that this appropriate choice of the exact word need not be a long, multi-syllable, "difficult" word.

> Conduct your blooming in the noise and whip of the
>   whirlwind
> (From "Sermon on the Warpland,"
> *In the Mecca*)

Blooming and whirlwind are concrete, visible, physical realities and because of their concreteness, we immediately recognize that each belongs to opposite categories of reality; in fact the nature and purpose of the whirlwind is to destroy all blooming. Thus Sister Brooks is able to make a very strong political comment without resorting to trite political cliches. The use of words which have physical, visible existence is often more powerful, more clear than abstractions like "the universe" and "the cosmos."

St. Julia, a character described by Sister Brooks in the poem "In the Mecca," is a "good" church-going sister who dearly loves Jesus. Sister Brooks has St. Julia cry out:

> He's the comfort and wine
> and piccalilli for my soul

Picalilli here is another extremely concrete word, simple word that reveals Sister Brooks' intimate knowledge of the black community's eating habits (picalilli being just the right topping for black-eye peas and rice/she didn't say "relish"). Through this word, we can make some very concrete deductions about where and how St. Julia grew up as well as how she feels about Jesus.

Awkward Rhythm and Rhyme

RHYTHM: Rhythm is achieved primarily by the alternation of stressed and unstressed syllables and by spacing on the page which imposes pauses at certain points. What this means for the poet as technician is that if his rhythms are going to be strong, he must learn how to say exactly what he wants to say (using images, the appropriate, exact choice of word, etc.) while at the same time juggling syllables. This is a very difficult thing to do. What sometimes happens with the poet who is beginning to write is that he gets so caught up with manipulating syllables that he subordinates his choice of words or limits his choice of words by emphasizing a stressed syllable. In achieving rhythm that is *both black* and *original*, the poet should try to move away from the sing/song effect of iambic tetrameter or iambic trimeter lines (de-dah, de-dah, de-dah, de-dah; or de-dah, de-hah, de-dah), especially when these rhythms are used with rhymed couplets or alternate rhyme (aa bb, or abab). Although an excellent poem in terms of color, imagery, Countee Cullen lessens the originality and effectiveness of his poem "Heritage" by the following sing/song rhythm and rhyme.

> What is Africa to me:
> Copper sun or scarlet sea,

> Jungle star or jungle track
> Strong bronzed men, or regal black

Amiri Baraka is a master at manipulating blackmusic rhythms. His rhythms are black and original in part because often they are based on other principles than having stressed syllables come at predictable intervals. Rather, Amiri creates internal rhyme as well as rhythm by repeating stressed *sounds* at intervals that are dictated by his feel for black liferhythms and blackmusic. For example, in the beginning of "The Nation Is Like Ourselves," from *It's Nation Time:*

> The nation is like ourselves, together
> seen in our various scenes, sets where ever we are
> what ever we are doing, is what the nation . . .

Key to the rhythm of these lines are the "s" sounds, the staccato sound of "where ever" and "what ever," and the alternation of staccato sounds with fluid sounds, sounds that flow instead of jump. What makes Amiri a master at what he is doing here is that his meaning, his appropriate choice of words is not subordinated to his rhythm, but rather they complement one another. Another excellent example of rhythms manipulated in a black/original manner is Robert Hayden's poem "Runagate, Runagate," which appears in Dudley Randall's anthology *Black Poetry.*

RHYME: Sometimes inexperienced poets think the only way to achieve rhyme is by alternating the last word of each line with another word that ends with the same sound. Also, as in the Countee Cullen example above, poets sometimes rely totally on couplets or alternate rhyme. Both of these rhyme schemes tend to have that sing/song effect. Gwendolyn Brooks and Amiri Baraka are two poets who make use of other rhyme schemes and who achieve internal rhyme through repetition of similar sounds within a line or several lines. Sister Brooks, in particular, is an excellent example of one who manipulates hard sounds, soft sounds within lines without in any way being mechanical in her choice of words or in any way limiting her meaning. She also sometimes uses off-rhyme, that is rhyming sounds at the end of lines which do not rhyme exactly. The following excerpt from "In the Mecca" is an example of a rhyme scheme other

than couplet and alternate rhyme, which is not trite and
sing/song:

> Briggs is adult as a stone
> (who if he cries cries alone).
> The Gangs are out, but he must go
> to and fro,
> appease what reticences move
> across the intemperate range.
> Immunity is forfeit, love
> is luggage, hope is heresy.
> Gang
> is health and mange.
> Gang
> is a bunch of ones and a singlicity.
> Please pity Briggs. But there is a central height in pity
> past which man's hand and sympathy cannot go;
> past which the little hurt dog
> descends to mass—no longer Joe,
> not Bucky, not Cap'n, not Rex,
> not Briggs—and is all self-employed,
> concerned with Other,
> not with Us. . . .

Some of Us Lack a Sense of Direction

Our ultimate reality wherever we may live on the face of
this earth is that we are Black and oppressed people. Everything
we do from what we eat to who and how we love is affected
by that ultimate reality. Thus we feel the poetry of Africans
(Black People) must reflect and deal with that reality. It is hard
to deal with Poetry that talks about how a young sister wants
to fall in love and be carried away into never-never land. The
hard fact is that we as a people have been taken to never-never
land and are still trying to adjust to that. Love poetry can be
written which talks of love and which gives direction to our
understanding of the conditions under which we live. A close
reading of Mari Evans' book *I Am A Black Woman* (especially
the title poem of that book), and Johari Amini's *Let's Go Some
Where* shows us that such blklove poetry can be produced, well.
Also, we feel that poetry which deals solely with the positive
attributes of nature, the sun, moon and stars is relevant to our

oppression. If a poet is to deal with nature, then perhaps he should deal with the reality that we have no land in the U.S.

Actually, directions come from the world you are involved in each and everyday. If your work is putting comic books together or is one of being a professional student you will see the world differently from a person working on the line at Ford Motor Co. We don't write about land and food or nature because we think that our food comes from A & P. Where do they get it? Suppose A & P closed. Question that and a whole new world opens up.

If what you are to give our people is to be meaningful, it must have some *relationship to reality.* And reality is not the same to the doer as it is to the sayer. There are four areas in which you should concentrate much of your efforts if you are to develop as a person and a writer:

1. *Study* and *Research:* This is of the utmost importance for the writers of non-fiction and certain kinds of fiction such as historical fiction. Margaret Walker's research for her novel *Jubilee* took almost a lifetime and Chancellor Williams's research for his monumental study, *The Destruction of Black Civilization,* took eighteen years. The two books mentioned will live because they are packed with life-giving and stimulating information written in a style that is readable.
2. *Writing:* Must be the major endeavor for the beginning writer. You should at first put yourself on a schedule in order to acquire discipline. Discipline in anything that you do is important and is a must for the writer. You are your own whip. Self-discipline is the hardest to achieve but if achieved may be your most important asset. Keep a small notebook with you, jot down all ideas, don't rely solely on memory. Don't throw any of the notes away. Keep the unused ones for later. You may want to concentrate in one area of writing but you should have *knowledge* of all areas—fiction, non-fiction, children, radio & television, magazine-journalism, poetry, drama, etc.
3. *Revision:* Never accept a first draft of your work. The art of writing is frequent revising. We must be our own worst critics. We must be our own editors.
4. *Workshop:* Good for the beginning and the inexperienced writer, mostly for the associations that are formed with other

writers. Re-enforcement in pain. Also, one of the few places you can probably get competent and truthful direct criticism. Many good writers have been involved in the workshop experience: Hoyt Fuller, Gwendolyn Books, John O. Killens, John H. Clarke, Sterling Plumpp, Johari Amini, we can go on and on.

The Hard Flower

Writing is a form of self-definition and communication through which you basically define yourself and your relationship to the world. The writer is essentially always searching for the core of the definition, looking for the gut. The truth. There are few good writers that lie; there are a lot of liars that try to write and unfortunately they are in the majority. But they come and go, passing through like a European wind penetrating the Afrikan heat only to be eliminated by the warmth of realness.

As we said earlier the writer is a questioner, always asking, always seeking the bottom line, always looking for the essences within the essence. Always looking for the enemies of the world. When the writer stops questioning, he stops having anything important to say. To question is to admit that you don't know everything. It's a posture, a relationship to the world that is conducive for creativity. *They who humble themselves before knowledge of any kind generally end up the wiser and as voices with something meaningful to say.*

A question that we would like to leave with you is: Why do you wish to become a writer at a time when most black people are not able to eat properly?

Final Words

You are a reflection of your people—regardless of what anybody says. If you are Black, you will always be Black first and a writer second. Understand this. Writing is a vocation, a job, a weapon, a psychological necessity to be used in the best interests of our people (which also means the world's people). Always take yourself and your work seriously although *not* too seriously. Learn to smile and always listen to our people, especially the elders. Do more listening than talking. Your talking will be done with the pen, pencil or typewriter. Have patience with yourself and with life—it is going to be very, very difficult. I guarantee that.

Haki R. Madhubuti (don l. lee)
Institute of Positive Education
Chicago, Ill.   3/1/75

Books I Would Recommend to the Beginning Writer:

The Destruction of Black Civilization, by Chancellor Williams. Third World Press, Chicago.
Report From Part One, By Gwendolyn Brooks. Broadside Press, Detroit.
A Broadside Treasury, ed. by Gwendolyn Brooks. Broadside Press.
Garvey, Lumumba, Malcolm: Black Nationalist-Separatists, by Shawna Maglanbayan. Third World Press.
Blackness and the Adventure of Western Culture, by George Kent. Third World Press.
How I Wrote Jubilee, by Margaret Walker. Third World Press.
After the Killing, by Dudley Randall. Third World Press.
An Afrikan Frame of Reference, by Johari Amini. Institute of Positive Education, Chicago.
The Present Is a Dangerous Place to Live, by Keorapetse Kgositsile. Third World Press.
Steps to Break the Circle, by Sterling Plumpp. Third World Press.
Homecoming, by Sonia Sanchez. Broadside Press.
A Blues Book for Blue Black Beautiful Women, by Sonia Sanchez. Broadside Press.
Holy Ghosts, by Ahmed Alhamisi. Broadside Press.
Re: Creation, by Nikki Giovanni. Broadside Press.
Black Velvet, by Everett Hoagland. Broadside Press.
Riot, by Gwendolyn Brooks. Broadside Press.
Journey to Afrika, by Hoyt Fuller. Third World Press.
Pamo-Ja-Tashinda, by Kalamu Ya Salaam. Ahidianana. New Orleans, La. 70125.
Hofu Ni Kwenu, by Kalamu Ya Salaam. Ahidianana.
From Plan to Planet: Life Studies: The Need for Afrikan Minds and Institutions, Haki Madhubuti. Broadside Press.
Book of Life, by Haki R. Madhubuti. Broadside Press.
This is just a partial listing of books that are important and are readily available from Black publishers. Study them, they will help you in your development as writers and as Black people.

Haki Madhubuti

DUDLEY RANDALL

Prologue

> What is a poet?
> A poet is one who writes poetry.
> Why do you want to be a poet? To become famous and
>   appear on TV?
> Then rob a bank. You'll be on the six o'clock news.
> To make money?
> Go into business. It's a surer way.
> To effect social change?
> Become a politician.

Poets write because they must. Because they have an inner drive. Whether or not any one hears of them, whether or not they make a cent, whether or not they affect a single person, poets write and will continue to write.

Poets' medium is language. Do you love words? The sound of them, the rhythm of them, their differences and similarities, the way they paint pictures, stir emotions? If you were a prisoner and wrote a letter, would you say, "I'm incarcerated," or would you say, "I'm in jail"? If you would say, "I'm in jail," then you are sensitive to words, and may be a poet. Read on.

The New Preparation

Often one meets people who say, "When I have five minutes I sit down and dash off a poem." One would not employ a surgeon or a house builder who says, "When I have five minutes I take a whatcha-call-em and dash off an operation or throw together a house." Each has undergone long and careful training so he can perform a skilled operation. Likewise, a poet should have intensive knowledge and practice of his art.

James Weldon Johnson in his *Book of American Negro Spirituals* reports that the persons who were most esteemed by the folk as leaders of folk singing were not necessarily those with the "best" voices. Often their voices were old and cracked, but these leaders had enormous knowledge of many folk songs. They had a vast repertory of lines and phrases and could always think of a verse to fit a particular occasion.

Likewise, Alex Haley, in his book *Roots* which tells of how he retraced his ancestors back to a Mandingo village, reveals how the griots had a vast memory of events and people going back hundreds of years. Even if these people did not have "book learning," they had learning. Poets also are part of a long tradition, which you should learn, either orally or in books.

Formerly, Black American poets were limited to what they learned in school. They learned about Whitman, Dickinson, Eliot, Pound, Williams, Shakespeare, Keats, Shelley, and Auden. But they learned little about their heritage of Black poetry. Or, if they learned, they had to learn it on their own. Now, with the flowering of Black Studies courses and Black publishers, they have greater access to their own sources of poetry.

You can learn about Black folk poetry in such books as James Weldon Johnson's *Book of American Negro Spirituals* or Talley's *Negro Folk Rhymes* and about both folk and literary black poetry in Sterling Brown's *Negro Caravan*, Dudley Randall's *The Black Poets*, and Xavier Nicholas's *The Poetry of Soul* and *Poetry of the Blues*.

There are many anthologies of Black poetry. Among them are LeRoi Jones and Larry Neal's *Black Fire*, Arnold Adoff's *The Poetry of Black America*, Richard Barksdale and Kenneth Kinamon's *Black American Poetry*, Richard Long and Eugenia Collier's *Black Poetry in America*. Poets should study the history of their literature in Saunders Redding's *To Make a Poet Black*, Sterling Brown's *American Negro Poetry*, Roger Whitlow's *Black American Literature*, and Charles P. Davis's *From the Dark Tower*.

You should read thoughtful books like W. E. B. Du Bois's *The Souls of Black Folk*, Frantz Fanon's *Black Faces, White Masks* and *The Wretched of the Earth*. Black poets should learn the background of their history by reading Chancellor Williams's *The Destruction of Black Civilization* and the books of Joel A. Rodgers, Ben Jochannon, and Chiek Anta Diop.

Stephen Henderson has a description of the unique qualities of Black poetry in his *Understanding the New Black Poetry*. Don Lee writes of the younger poets in *Dynamite Voices: Black Poets of the 1960's*. Bernard Bell reveals similarities in folk and literary poetry in *The Folk Roots of Afro-American Poetry*.

You can also learn about Black poetry not only in books, but by listening to the talk you hear all around you in the street, in the home, in bars, churches, from preachers, old folks, children, adolescents, men in varied trades and professions. All these are sources of living speech, which the poet hears and remembers and turns into poetry.

You should listen to music, all types of music, including in addition to classical music such folk music as blues, spirituals, ballads, gospel songs, children's and vendors' chants. As well as suggesting sound effects to incorporate into your poetry, they can suggest structure, mood, and tone, which you can use in your poems.

Special study should be given to Black folk poetry, for it is characterized by compression, directness, simplicity, clarity, and striking images which help to make strong poetry.

Study of a foreign literature will broaden you and give you a perspective on poetry written in your own language. In short, you should open yourself to all of life, to all experiences, to all of mankind, to the whole rich bustling wonderful world, which you will transmute into poetry.

Aims

I suppose by "Aims" is meant what you intend to do with your poetry, or the effect you wish your poetry to have on your audience. To answer these questions requires introspection, self-examination, as I suggest in my "Prologue." You may write poetry for a variety of reasons; you may wish to influence your audience in various ways. Fame, wealth, notoriety, power, I consider as insufficient motivations for writing poetry. The best motivation for writing poetry, I believe, is that something inside you, some demon, some possession, compels you to write. My happiest moments have been those in which I was writing. Yet writing is something more than therapy, self-gratification. When a poet publishes his work, he expects it to do something for his readers.

This brings up the question of ideology, or teaching. The poet's own experiences, I think, will determine how overtly didactic he will be. I can understand how a South African poet, for instance, escaping from that oppressive regime, will write of nothing but the need for liberation. In my own case, however, I was a preacher's son, and heard too much preaching at home. I believe that readers instinctively resist a writer who has an obvious design on them, who too obviously tries to manipulate them. The salesman knocks on our door with his sample case in his hand, and we immediately think of excuses not to buy . . .

However, if a poet is moved, not by a narcissistic desire to appear on television, but by some powerful experience, he may wish to share it with others. One virtue of poetry is that it makes us more alive, more perceptive, wakes up our sleeping senses. Reading Margaret Danner's poetry, for instance, with its discrimination of different textures, awakes us to a keener sensitivity to the world around us. She wrote a poem comparing carnations to gardenias, calling one masculine and the other feminine because of their texture. We had formerly confused, confounded the two flowers as just white and round, but her subtle discrimination makes us look more closely at these flowers and see their differences. She makes us more alive to the world around us.

The press of business and the tendency to abstract keeps us from really seeing the world, makes us reduce it to cliched abstractions. We see a white man, a Negro, a Jew, a woman. Instantly there springs to mind some abstract stereotype, instead of our scrutinizing the person and trying to understand a unique individual different from all the three billion other individuals on earth. This is the virtue of poetry, that it goes back to the primitive radical roots of language, and makes us live in the poem, not move abstract counters, such as honkie, nigger, Jew, broad. If we could feel how even a pin prick hurts, then we would not be so apt to consign whole populations to death: "the final solution," "drive them into the sea," "the yellow peril," "put the nigger in his place," "the only good Indian is a dead Indian."

This is not to say that the poet should not have beliefs or ideology, but that he should not bully the reader with them. If the reader likes and respects the poet, he will unconsciously absorb his attitudes, especially if they are couched in memorable language. Poetry delights, and through delight it moves to wisdom as someone has said before.

This delight is one of the most important, though often unconscious, aims of poetry. We live on earth not knowing why we are here, where we came from or where we are going. In our brief stay we feel joy, sorrow, pain, hope and fear. The poet takes this mystery, these varied emotions and puts them into a form which gives us

joy and delight, joy and delight, poems
conceived in joy, endowing the world and time
with joy and delight, joy and delight, for ever.

Subject Matter

"Nothing human is alien to me." I believe that is sufficient.

Method

Method could mean many things, the manner of writing, or
how to get ideas, or how to sell your work. I have decided to
write here about how to market your work, for most writers
want to communicate to others, and in order to communicate
their work must be sold, or at least accepted, and then distributed.

A common mistake is to send your work to publications which
do not use that type of work. Broadside Press, for instance,
is interested in poetry, but we receive many novels, plays, and
sometimes Ph.D. dissertations on such subjects as "Black In-
Migration into Dorset County between 1910 and 1920." Of course
such submissions are promptly returned. This waste of time could
have been avoided if the writers had studied the publications
of Broadside Press and learned what we customarily publish.

It's a good idea to go to your bookstore, drugstore, or public
library and check their magazines. Find out which ones publish
poetry. Study more than one issue of those which publish poetry,
and learn what kind of poetry they publish. Do they publish
poetry by Blacks; poetry in traditional forms such as sonnets,
ballades, villanelles, rondeaux, rondels, triolets, canzoni, haiku,
cinquaims, blank verse; experimental poetry; free verse; concrete
poetry? When you find magazines which publish verse similar
to the kind you write, then submit your work to those publications.

There are many publications which publish poetry. One can
find them listed in *Directory of Small Presses and Magazines,
Writer's Market, Writer's Digest, The Writer, Writers' Handbook.*
Dudley Randall's *The Black Poets* has an appendix listing period-
icals which publish Black poetry.

Don't compromise yourself by trying to slant your work toward
a particular magazine. Write as well as you can in the manner
which is natural to you, then submit your work to the magazines
which publish that type of work.

In submitting your work, bear in mind that you will be
competing against hundreds of other writers, many of whom

are professionals. It's elementary that your work should be neatly typed, not mimeographed or xeroxed, one poem to a page, correctly spelled, in good grammar, with your name and address on each page, and accompanied by a stamped, self-addressed return envelope. If you don't supply envelope and return postage, the editor has no obligation to return your work.

Don't betray your amateur status by asking about copyright. You can learn about copyright by research at your public library, or by writing the Copyright Office, Washington, D.C. 20504, for free pamphlets on literary copyright. Don't appear to be a kook or a paranoiac by hinting that someone will steal your material. If you believe that, don't send it out.

A letter of transmittal is not necessary. If you must send one, make it brief and to the point. Letters may subliminally turn the editor against your work, especially if you can't spell or don't know the difference between *to* and *too, lie* and *lay, who's* and *whose, its* and *it's, lend* and *loan, there* and *their.* My heart always sinks when I receive a letter from a prisoner who says, "I'm incarcerated" instead of "I'm in jail." His diction reveals he doesn't know the principle of economy, and uses swollen language.

If you've made some of the mistakes listed above, your work will be returned to you almost immediately. If you have heard nothing about your work for three months, send the editor a letter with a return envelope requesting the return of your material unless he has decided to publish it. In most cases this will ensure its prompt return.

Most small magazines have insufficient staff to read the large number of poems they receive. There are only a few good poems and many bad ones, and on these it isn't hard to make a decision. There are, however, poems of middling quality about which the editor has doubts and which he may hold in order to make a decision. A letter requesting their return will probably tip his mind to a decision to return them.

One thing you should never do, if you are considerate, is to request that an editor comment on your poems. To do so is to confuse an editor with a teacher. The job of an editor is to select poems for his magazine, not to teach people how to write. He receives hundreds of poems and in order to report on them as promptly as possible he encloses a politley worded rejection slip. That is all the professional writer requires. He knows his poem is not accepted by magazine A and he promptly sends it to magazine B. If the editor had to explain why he rejected each poem, it would take much more of his limited time, and writers would receive reports on their work much later than they do now. There are many places where writers can obtain comments on their work. They can enroll in creative writing classes, they can take correspondence courses, they can organize or join local writers' workshops, they can attend writers' conferences. It is there, and not from editors, that they should ask for comments on their work.

The question arises whether a poet should first try to publish single poems or should wait until he has a book ready for publication. I think that a poet should first send out single poems, or groups of two or three poems, for publication first. In that way he learns about the markets for poetry, acquires experience by perhaps making some of the mistakes listed above and learning from them, and if his poems are published, he brings them to the attention of the public and of editors. If he outgrows his poems, they will have been published only in ephemeral publications like magazines, and will not be permanently exposed in books. I know several poets who published books prematurely, and were embarrassed by them later.

To keep track of your poems, keep a notebook and record where and when you send each poem, and what happens to it. Here is an example:

Title	Sent	Date	Fate	Date	Published	Price	Next
"Love"	BLACK WORLD	5/10/72	Returned				Jrnl of Blk Poetry
"Love"	Jrnl of Blk Poetry	7/13/72	Accepted	8/23/72 1/15/73		$0	ESSENCE

Notice, in the above form, you decide where next to send the poem in the event it's returned. This insures that you always have something in the mail and keeps you from feeling depressed, for as soon as a poem is returned you mail it out and always have something to hope for.

When a poem is published, enter it on a 3 × 5 card to keep your bibliography up to date. In the event you need to write a resume or list your published works, you will have a complete, accurate file of your published works. Example:

Jones, Ray—Bibliography—Poems
"Love" (poem) JOURNAL OF BLACK POETRY, Vol. 1, No. 15. Winter 1973. page 72.

The Hard Flower

Miss Brooks's title for this section seems paradoxical. Flowers are soft, not hard. I take it to mean, however, that your finished product will have the beauty of a flower, but will also have the capacity to endure, like brass or marble.*

How do you make your poems endure? Or, in other words, how do you keep them alive in the mouths of men? Naturally, men will repeat words whose meaning is important to them. Therefore, you must infuse your words with meaning. But that depends on the quality of your mind. In this context, we are speaking not of the quality of your mind, but of the technical means of causing men to remember and repeat your words. Men will repeat and remember words if they are arranged in a way which makes it easy for them to remember and repeat the words. In this context, languages differ. Let us compare English with Latin:

> Boy loves girl.
> Puer amat puellam.

Both sentences mean the same thing. But reverse them.

> Girl loves boy.
> Puellam amat puer.

Here, the sentences have different meanings. The Latin still means the same thing—Boy loves girl, whereas in the English sentence the action is reversed. That is because of the different genius of the English and Latin languages, which gives them different capabilities. Latin is an inflected language. The meaning and relationship of words change with the inflections of the words. English, except for the plural and the possessive, (girls, girl's, girls'), is an uninflected language. Changes in the meaning and relationships of words are indicated by their position in the sentence, not by changes in the word. The normal, idiomatic order of words in an English sentence is subject, verb, object: Boy loves girl. Therefore, English-speaking people will remember and repeat such an arrangement of words most naturally and

---

*Editor's note: means that the *black* poem will be beautiful as a flower is beautiful, but will have a spine of black strength.

easily. Many memorable lines have been composed in that arrangement: "We bake de bread,/They give us de crust;" "Ripeness is all;" "(He) drank his blood and ate his heart."

If you want your lines to be remembered, arrange the words in the normal, idiomatic manner of the English language—subject, verb, object—Boy loves girl. Then people will find them easy to repeat and remember. Do not write long involved sentences which confuse and puzzle the reader. You weaken your style in this way. A good model to study and learn from is the Negro secular song included in the autobiography of Frederick Douglass and reprinted in *The Negro Caravan* and *The Black Poets:* "We bake de bread,/They give us de crust."

In Latin, on the other hand, words can be shifted with great flexibility, since it is their endings, not their position in the sentence, which determine their relationships with other words. The two most conspicuous positions in a sentence are the beginning and the end. In poetry, where each sentence may be divided into separate lines, there are additional conspicuous positions, the beginning and the end of each *line.* Because of the flexibility of the Latin language, a Latin poet could compose his poem like a mosaic, placing a word here, a word there, like a red or a blue tile, according to the effect he wanted to achieve. If he wanted to emphasize the girl, he could say, *Puellam* amat puer. If he wanted to emphasize the act, he could say, *Amat* puer puellam. If he wanted to emphasize the boy, he could say, *Puer* amat puellam. He could also secure emphasis by varying the last word in the sentence. A writer in English is much more restricted in that regard. He can obtain emphasis by varying the normal word order, but he may be called inept, old-fashioned, archaic, literary, or Latinate. He must be sure the reversal is for expressiveness, not to satisfy the exigencies of meter or rime. In "The Southern Road" I began a line with "Love you I must." Margaret Danner objected to the inversion. I explained that I wanted to emphasize the love, but she insisted that I keep the natural word order. So I changed it "I have to love you." I don't know whether I gained or lost by the change. One must weigh surprise, expressiveness, and force against being natural.

Since the beginning is a prominent position, the title of a poem is important. Calling a poem "Untitled" is a lazy cop-out. A title is a handle to a poem. Often poems called "Untitled" are identified by their first line, or a line or a phrase taken from the body of the poem. The author could have identified the poem in the first place. Sometimes the meaning or explanation of a poem will depend on the title. Often we can look at the Contents of a book of poems and apprehend the essence of the book. The titles may reflect nature, or places, or people, or history. A table of contents with titles about blackness or revolution will suggest the character of the book. The poetic quality of the titles suggests the quality of the poems. Think of the titles of the Spirituals, some poetic, some dramatic: "Deep River;" "Sometimes I Feel Like a Motherless Child;" "Gamblin' Man Get Off Your Knees;" "Joshua Fit the Battle of Jericho."

You should avoid telling the reader what form the poem is, like entitling it "Sonnet," which hints that the reader doesn't know what a sonnet is. The poet should let the reader discover that the poem is a sonnet or a ballade, or, if the reader doesn't know what a sonnet or a ballade is, the poet should let the form work its peculiar magic on the reader. For that reason, I didn't call "The Southern Road" "Ballade of the Southern Road." As far as I know, no critic, book reviewer, or poet has noticed that the poem is a ballade, but I think nevertheless the form works its unique effect upon the reader.

Likewise, first lines are important. They lead the reader into the poem. They may hook his interest and stimulate him to read further, or turn him away from the poem. A critic renewed interest in Walt Whitman by writing an essay composed of quotations of his striking initial lines and other lines of beauty or power. If a book has an index of first lines, you can get an idea of the quality of the poetry by scanning the lines, and you may be attracted to a poem by its beautiful first line. First lines may be personal and dramatic: "For Godsake hold your tongue and let me love." Or imaginative: "I saw eternity the other night." Or challenging: "If we must die, let us not die like hogs." Or boldly contrasting: "First fight, then fiddle." Or strikingly rhythmic: "Out of the cradle endlessly rocking." There are countless way to entice the reader into the poem with a striking first line.

Just as the beginning of a poem is conspicuous, the end of a poem is important. It's the last impression a reader has of a poem, and it should leave a memorable one. David Diop has some memorable last lines. The whole force of the poem seems concentrated in them. Read his poems and study his concluding lines, like these:

O I am lonely so lonely here. "The Renegade"
The bitter taste of liberty. "Africa"
Rise up and shout: NO! "Defiance Against Force"

In addition to writing striking and memorable titles, first lines, and concluding lines, make every line between the first and the last lines as good as they are, and you'll have it made.

This brings up the question of what a good line of poetry is, and how you write a good line. If we all knew what a good line of poetry is, and were able to write them, we'd all be great poets. First of all, if we live with great lines of poetry, read them, think about them, repeat them to ourselves, we may be able to absorb some of their power, and set it forth in our own writings. People who read the Bible, who know the Bible, who ponder it and try to live by it, often attain a beauty of expression. That is because the Bible is a great piece of literature as well as a great religious work. Many people who were not well educated and who knew few books beyond the Bible, yet were able to speak and write with eloquence because they had absorbed some of the beauty of that Book. Think of the songs of the slave singers.

You can absorb something from the world's great poetry. Genius is not restricted to any nation or any race. Read English, Swahili, Latin, Russian, Greek, Arabic, Chinese, French, Spanish, Italian, any language which your liking, curiosity, or circumstances permits you to learn. Remember their great lines of poetry, repeat them to yourself, apply them to your daily living, and use them as touchstones to judge your lines and the lines of others you may read.

The question still arises: How do you know a good line? A good line is one which you remember without trying, whose phrasing is inevitable. What it says is said so well that there is no other way to say it better. One thing that makes it easy to remember is for it to be in the natural idiom and word order of the language: in English, in the word order of subject, verb, object, or, Boy loves girl. Analyze any good line of poetry and you will see that its syntax is clear; you don't have to worry about what the subject, or the verb, or the object is. You know what they are without having to puzzle over them. In addition, what is said is memorable, is worth while. By negative definition, lines like

a

the

in

to

are not memorable. What comfort or knowledge or inspiration or enjoyment can you get from lines like these? How can you remember lines like these? Yet some poets write such lines and call them lines of poetry. Such lines do not even have rhythm, since they are composed of solitary unaccented syllables. One of the prime requisites of poetry is sound, since poetry is a vocal not a visual art, and one of the components of the ordered sound of poetry is rhythm. In order to have rhythm, there must be a basis of comparison. One sound does not make rhythm, for there is nothing to compare it to. The heart beats once. No rhythm. It beats again, and there is rhythm. We can say it beats fast or slowly because we can compare one beat to another. Moreover, when the poets read such lines aloud, they do not read them as distinct separate lines, but run them into the other lines. Since they run them into the other lines, they should have been run into the other lines on the page, as poetry should be written down to indicate the way it sounds, not for the way it looks upon the page. We must learn to notate our poems correctly. Unless we learn to notate our poems correctly, the reader will have no way of knowing how they should be read.

We can discern two principles by which things are remembered, contrast and similarity. In a crowd, you remember a pair of twins, dressed alike, the same age, height, weight. You also remember a strikingly dissimilar pair, like a giant and a dwarf. Likewise, we remember lines of poetry by their contrast:

Fools rush in where angels fear to tread.

where the contrast is between fools and angels, rush in and fear to tread. Or we remember the similarity (repetition) of

Black love is black wealth.

Sometimes there is a combination of contrast and similarity, as in:

First fight, then fiddle

where there is the contrast between fight and fiddle, which is heightened by the similarity of the alliteration of the *f*'s. The same combination of contrast and similarity is seen in

*k*ill with *k*indness.

Sometimes lines are remembered just for their human emotional qualities, as the tenderness of

I will be more
having known your love.

or the kindliness of

and kept each other warm

or the menace of

will the machine gunners please step forward

although here there is the latent contrast of the deadliness of the machine gunners and the politeness of the word "please."

It would be helpful to read poems which you admire, to notice which lines remain in your memory, analyze them to see why you remember them, repeat them, live with them, and use them as touchstones for judging others' lines and your own lines. Gradually, just as the beauty of the Bible pervades the language of those who read it frequently, the beauty of those touchstone lines which you remember will creep into the lines you write.

For an example of how to use lines as touchstones to judge poetry, to sharpen your critical faculties, and to revise your poems, compare one of the lines quoted (For Godsake hold your tongue and let me love) with another line quoted (a).

The first line uses normal idiomatic word order (subject, verb, object: boy loves girl): hold your tongue . . . let me love, which makes the line easy to understand and to remember. The music reinforces the sense because the cadence is rapid and the gutteral alliterations *G*odsa*k*e . . . tongue and the liquid alliterations *l*et me *l*ove harmonize with the different demands. The contrast between "shut up" and "love" also makes the line memorable.

On the other hand, the second line (a) has no meaning, and is vague, vapid, vacant, and valueless. You should strike out the line "a" or place the "a" where it belongs, with its noun. This is an extreme comparison, but such testing of lines will sharpen your critical faculties and enable you to spot weaknesses in your poetry and revise them.

It is not only the meaning or syntactical form of lines that makes them memorable, but also the sound, since poetry is a vocal art.

English poetry is patterned by rhythm, measured by stressed and unstressed syllables. Quantity, or duration of sounds, is also used, especially by black poets (We a baddDDD people) but not in regular patterns. Metrists could describe many different rhythms of stressed and unstressed syllables, but the basic rhythms are iambic, trochaic, anapestic, and dactyllic. Iambic rhythm consists of one unstressed syllable followed by one stressed syllable, as in "befóre." This is called one iambic foot. Rhythmical units are called feet from the fact that the earliest poetry was combined with music and dance. (In Africa, even today, music, poetry, and dance go together.) The line can be lengthened by adding additional feet, making the length two, three, four, five, or even eight feet. Generally, after eight feet, the line is shortened by splitting it into shorter lines.

> Before/ the smile/ of day

is a line of three iambic feet.

Trochaic rhythm is iambic rhythm reversed, one accented syllable followed by one unaccented syllable.

> After / twilight / laughter

This is a line of three trochaic feet.

Anapestic rhythm is two unaccented syllables followed by one accented syllable. Since English has many particles—unaccented monosyllables like articles (a, an, the) and prepositions (to, of, in, for, etc.) these particles are often joined with nouns or adjectives to compose anapestic feet.

> At the beau/tiful smile / of the day

This is a line of three anapestic feet.

Dactyllic rhythm is the opposite of anapestic rhythm. It consists of one accented syllable followed by two unaccented syllables:

Beautiful / mystery
Wonderful / history

Each of these lines contains two dactyllic feet. Notice the different emotional effects of the different rhythms.

There is one more rhythm, the spondaic, but it is not used throughout complete poems. It consists of two accented syllables:

Fáts Dómino

Since there are almost no English words with two consecutive accented syllables, spondees are used only sporadically. They occur when a monosyllable and the accented syllable of a longer word are juxtaposed, as above, or when two monosyllables occur together:

Which hints the whole by showing the párt cléar

To get the feel of the various rhythms, write poems in each rhythm, first with lines of one foot, then with lines of two, three, four, five, and six feet in each line. Then you can combine rhythms. The line previously quoted, "Out of the cradle endlessly rocking," uses alternate dactyllic and trochaic feet. In your practice poems, do not let the necessity of riming or of maintaining rhythm force you to alter the natural idiomatic order of words to to use words which don't make sense or which don't precisely express your meaning. It's the mark of a true poet that he can compose words in a beautiful and memorable form and still make them appear artless, spontaneous, and natural.

Free verse, which is used widely today, is verse without regular patterns of rhythm or rime. This does not mean that a contemporary poet must dispense with rhythm or rime. He can use them in his free forms to suggest the meaning. He can emphasize ideas by introducing pattern, as when Etheridge Knight emphasizes two lines in his free verse poem "Hard Rock Returns to Prison" by using rime:

And then the jewel of a myth that Hard Rock had once
bit

A screw on the thumb and poisoned him with syphilitic
spit.

Those poets who ridicule traditional verse by saying it goes
monotonously "da-dum, da-dum, da-dum" either have wooden
ears or do not know how to read aloud. Because of the different
weights of vowels and the easy-to-pronounce and hard-to-pro-
nounce combinations of consonants in the English language, there
are immense variations in the speed, quantity, tone color, and
pitch of lines, to say nothing of the variations in volume, pitch,
pause, tempo dictated by meaning. The "da-dum" is only an
understood pattern, like the 4/4 beat in music, against which
you can play innumerable variations. The best writers of free
verse are those skilled in traditional verse, but many writers
write bad free verse because they never learned to write tradi-
tional verse.

Poetry Today

My view of poetry today is optimistic. Not only are poets
scattered over the whole country, instead of being concentrated
in Chicago or New York, but they are constantly moving, teaching
and learning in new places. Stephany moved from Chicago to
Berkeley to Chicago, Baraka from New York to San Francisco
to Newark, Margaret Danner from Chicago to Detroit to Rich-
mond to Memphis to Chicago, Ishmael Reed from Buffalo to
Berkeley. Also, the poets are stretching and growing. In their
recent books Hayden, Madhubuti, Baraka, Brooks showed change
and growth. Because of the emergence of Black bookstores and
publishers, poets no longer have to depend on Random House
or Morrow to be published. The older poets like Hayden, Brooks,
Walker, and Sterling Brown are still producing, and act as guides
and inspiration for younger poets.

In my own poetry, I no longer strive for the intricate, sonorous
stanzas of "The Southern Road." I try for a looser form, a more
colloquial diction, as in "Frederick Douglass and the Slave Break-
er." I want my poems to be read and understood by children,
students, farmers, factory workers, professors. I seek directness
and lucidity, but also a richness so that the reader will find
added meanings on each new reading. I avoid eccentricities and
grotesqueries. P. J. Conkwright speaking on typography in
Scholarly Publishing, 1972, has said what I feel about the content
of typography:

Looking back now on those Excelsior Press days
(from the advantage of time and distance) I
know that when I chose the fancy Ronaldson I
chose the worst body type of the three
before me. It was the worst because it
had the most distractions in it. The
little spur serifs constantly reminded
the reader: 'Look how elegant I am.'
It was what Elmer Adler used to call
a 'mannered' type. By 'mannered' he
meant that the type showed eccentric
peculiarities that detracted from
thought conveyance. It had mannerisms—
like eye twitching, or stuttering, or
elaborate gesturing. It's almost axi-
omatic that a good, readable type is an
invisible type. Invisible in the sense
that it never conspicuously makes its
presence known. It's not too lean and
not too fat. It has no mannerisms.
It's invisible.

I said almost the same thing in my poem "Aim," in *More to Remember:*

Bodied in words transparent as the air,
Which hint the whole by showing the part clear.

RECOMMENDED PUBLICATIONS

Books

Brown, Sterling Allen, ed. *The Negro Caravan.* New York, Arno Press, 1969. (Reprint of the 1941 edition.)
   The most complete anthology of Negro literature up to 1940. Includes folk poetry and prose and the early poems of Robert Hayden, which he will not allow to be reprinted now.
Jones, LeRoi, and Neal, Larry, eds. *Black Fire: an Anthology of Afro-American Writing.* New York, Morrow, 1968.
   This is to the literature of the 1960s what *The Negro Caravan*

was to earlier literature. Contains poetry, essays, short stories, and plays which discard white standards and reach for black criteria.

Henderson, Stephen. *Understanding the New Black Poetry*. New York, Morrow, 1973.

Examines Black poetry in the framework of Black speech, Black music, and the Black experience.

Shapiro, Karl. *A Prosody Handbook*. New York, Harper, 1965.

There are many handbooks on versification. This is one by a skilled contemporary poet, who maintains that the sound of words, as well as their denotations, should express the poet's meaning.

Smith, Chard Powers. *Pattern and Variation in Poetry*. New York, Scribner's, 1932.

Each poet has his favorite handbook. This was Robert Hayden's.

Strunk, William. *The Elements of Style*. New York, Macmillan, 1972.

The basis of a good poetic style is a good prose style. In this brief textbook Strunk tells you how to write with clarity and concision.

Talley, Thomas Washington, comp. *Negro Folk Rhymes, Wise and Otherwise*. Port Washington, N.Y., Kennikat Press, 1922.

A good collection of secular Black folk poetry.

Webster's New Collegiate Dictionary. Springfield, Mass., Merriam, 1974.

A convenient desk dictionary. You should also have a small paperback one which you can carry in your pocket and, like Malcolm X, read from aardvark to zygote.

Wells, Henry Willis. *Poetic Imagery*. New York, Columbia University Press, 1924.

Wells classifies metaphors by their imaginative qualities. This will make you sensitive to the imaginative values of images.

Periodicals

Black World, March 1975.

The whole issue focuses on Black publishing. It has an annotated directory of Black book publishers and an article on preparing the professional book manuscript.

Gerald, Carolyn F. "The Black Writer and His Role." *Negro Digest,* January 1969, p. 42–48.

Carolyn Gerald shows how language has been used to denigrate Black people by such words as "blacklist," "black ball," "black-mail," and tells how Black writers can combat this tendency.

Henderson, Stephen. "Saturation: Progress Report on a Theory of Black Poetry." *Black World,* June 1975, p. 4–17.

Henderson further develops his theory of saturation in the Black experience as one of the criteria for evaluating Black poetry.

Rodgers, Carolyn M. "Black Poetry—Where It's At." *Negro Digest,* September 1969, p. 16–17.

In this and the following essay Carolyn Rodgers describes the language, themes and genres of Black poets and gives them her own terminology.

————. "Breakforth, in Deed." *Black World,* September 1970, p. 13–22.

QUESTIONS AND ANSWERS

The following questions are asked frequently in letters from beginning poets to Broadside Press. The answers are by Dudley Randall, Broadside Press editor.

1. Q. I am a fifteen year old high school student and have been writing poetry for one year. How do I go about having a book published?

A. How fortunate that you became a poet so early! You have many years of writing ahead of you, so it's not necessary to rush into the permanence of book format. Some poets, Robert Hayden among them, published books very young, and now they don't want their juvenile publications to be seen. I asked Hayden for permission to reprint a poem from his first book, *Heartshape in the Dust,* and he said, "No, *no,* No, NO, *NO!* I wrote those poems in my apprentice years, when I was learning to write, and I don't want any of them reprinted." This period of learning how to write, discovering new poets, experimenting with new forms, can be one of your most enjoyable. Don't terminate it prematurely.

Read, read, read. And write, write, write. Don't try for book publication until you have published extensively in magazines and newspapers. Mari Evans was well-known for her contributions to magazines and anthologies before she published her first book. Such publication will be an indication that many different editors have found your work acceptable. Then publishers, perhaps, will have seen your poems somewhere, and will be more willing to risk from $500 to $10,000 on a first book by you, than on a book by an unknown poet. All the poems you sent me were in rimed couplets, which are only one of many forms and which have their limitations. Master the scores of other forms which you will find in Karl Shapiro's *A Prosody Handbook* or in any handbook on versification. Also, learn correct spelling and grammar. When you have learned the rules, you can break them, if you have good reasons to. After you have done these things, you can start sending your poems to magazines. Choose publications where the competition is not too tough, like your local newspaper, your school newspaper or yearbook, literary magazine, or your church bulletin. After mastering spelling, grammar, and forms, you will be ready to be published, but try ephemeral publications first, not the permanence of books, which you may regret later. Have fun!

2. Q. I have a teacher who reads and criticizes my poems. He says they are full of cliches. What can I do?

A. One of the best ways to learn to write is to have your work read and criticized by a competent person. You must develope a thick skin to criticism, and the ability to evaluate it objectively and apply it to your work to make it better. Praise only flatters your ego, but searching criticism exposes your flaws and points out what you must do to write better. Cliches are expressions which have been worked to death and have lost their freshness, surprise, and power, like "right on," "pigs," "Queen of the Nile," "Amerikkka," "sweet as a rose." Perhaps the reason you use cliches is that you have not read enough to observe their repetition. Read more widely and develope the knack of spotting over-used expressions and eliminate them from your writing.

3. Q. I want to send you my poems. Should I have them copyrighted first?

A. Literary work cannot be copyrighted until *after* publication. While it is in your possession it is protected by common law. Always keep a carbon copy of whatever you send out. To be copyrighted it must first be published with a copyright notice (Copyright © 1975 by John Doe) in a prominent place. Publication without this notice puts your work in the public domain and you lose all control over reprint rights. After publication, fill out a copyright registration form (form A, obtained from Copyright Office, Library of Congress, Washington, D.C. 20504), have it notarized, and mail it with $6 and two copies of your publication to the Copyright Office. They will mail you a certificate of registration.

Most publishers copyright the book in the author's name. Periodicals copyright each issue under the periodical, but on request will release all rights subsequent to first serial rights. To learn more about copyright, ask your librarian for a book on the subject, or write to the Copyright Office for free pamphlets. Always keep a carbon copy of your manuscript, and enclose a SASE (Self Addressed Stamped Envelope) with it. Otherwise the editor is not obligated to return your manuscript.

4. Q. If you don't publish my book, I'll publish it myself. How do I go about this?

A. I'm trying to publish only four books a year. This year I've published twelve. So I'm afraid that I can't take your book. In publishing your book, avoid vanity publishers. They'll charge you an exorbitant amount to print your book, and won't actively promote it, since they will have already made their profit from the printing charges. Go to an honest, competent printer in your home town. Discuss the book with him. He can suggest ways to print it inexpensively and attractively. The burden of selling it will be upon you. Estimate your audience. First, family. Then, friends. Then, groups to which you belong: your church, your school, your lodge, your clubs, your office, factory, or labor union. People cannot buy your book if they are unaware of its existence, so you must let the public know of your book. Beware of space advertising. It's too expensive and doesn't get results. Announcements to selected groups such as those above are more productive. List your book in bibliographical publications such as *Books in Print,* which will list your book by author, title, subject, and publisher for a small fee. Send copies to *Publisher's Weekly* for its Weekly Record. Both addresses are 1180 Avenue of the Americas, New York City 10036. Send copies to magazines and newspapers for review. Send a copy to the *Cumulative Book Index,* H. W. Wilson Co., 150 University Place, Bronx, N.Y. 10037. If you have a reporter or editor friend, get him to write an article about your book. Send copies to radio or television talk shows and ask to be interviewed. Books with information on publishing are *How to Publish, Promote and Sell Your*

Book, $2.00, Adams Press, and *The Publish-It-Your-self Handbook,* edited by Bill Henderson, $4.00, Pushcart Book Press.

5. Q. I think Don Lee's poems are outtasight. I've rewritten his best ones to make them even better. Do you want to see them?

    A. I'm afraid you've committed the greatest literary sin—plagiarism—using another author's material. It's all right to imitate or paraphrase a writer for practice, to learn sentence structure or figures of speech, but don't send out your imitations. If you do, you'll be whitelisted by every editor in the country. Don't be afraid to take the risk of being original, instead of playing it safe by imitating someone already successful.

6. Q. I'm an actress and elocutionist and have read my poems in public to great applause. May I come to your office and read them to you?

    A. Your photograph shows you're a person of great charm and beauty. The trouble is, those qualities might distract me from paying attention to the poetry. Suppose I didn't like

your poems, what could I say? It would be very embarrassing. The best way to get a poem evaluated is to mail it in, and let it be judged on its own merits.

7. Q. Why are your rejection slips so vague? You returned my poem but didn't tell me what was wrong with it. How can I learn to write better unless you point out my mistakes?

    A. An editor's job is not to teach you how to write, but to select poems for his publication. If editors criticized every poem they received, they'd have no time to edit their magazines. To learn to write, attend classes in creative writing, take correspondence courses, attend writers' conferences and workshops, form a writers' group among your friends and read and discuss your work, study books on writing, read criticism, read poets old and new, and write, write, write. Rejection slips are a tender subject. It seems that none of them please all writers. One writer objects because an editor corrects his work. Other writers complain when editors make no comment. Some writers argue for years when an editor has taken the time to make comments. There are so many varying reasons why a poem cannot be used that the safest thing is just to say politely that the poem is not for us and to return it. A professional writer will take the rejection in stride, examine the poem and perhaps revise it, and send it to another magazine. An amateur will agonize.

8. Q. I want to send my poems out, but am afraid they will be stolen. What can I do?
A. If you believe an editor is dishonest, don't send him your work. Wait until you find an honest editor, or publish it yourself. Editors have enough problems, and a suspicious poet is too much. Most poems an editor receives he is only too glad to return. The exceptional good poem, he is glad to publish. See also the answer to question 3.

9. Q. I have over 200 poems. Where can I get them published?
A. Don't burden an editor by sending him 200 poems. Select your best poems, and send them to the most likely markets. Study the *Directory of Little Magazines* at your library, pick out the most compatible titles, send for sample copies (pay the editor; he'll appreciate it),

and send your best poems to the magazine which publishes your kind of poetry. Study additional sources: *Writer's Market, Writer's Handbook, Writer's Digest, The Writer.* The Perspectives section of *Black World* lists new magazines. Try them, they may need material. The March 1975 issue of *Black World* is devoted to publishing, and has a list of Black publishers, and an article on how to prepare your manuscript for submission. Dudley Randall's *The Black Poets* lists Black publishers and Black periodicals in the appendix, although some of the magazines like *Black Dialogue, Liberator, Soulbook,* and *Tan* have ceased publication. Bill Katz's periodicals column in *Library Journal* lists new periodicals, and *Poetry* magazine also carries notices of new poetry magazines. Some Black periodicals which publish poetry are *Black World, Black Books Bulletin, Essence, Encore, Phylon, Negro History Bulletin, Crisis, Broadside Series, Obsidian, Hoodoo, Journal of Black Poetry, Yardbird Reader.* Remember that quality is more important than quantity and send only your best poems, and put your very best on top.

Friend.

c Walking with you ~~~~~~~~~~
c Shuts off shivering.

c Here we are.
c Here we are.
~~Now it is not November~~

It is June; it is April or the best of October
I am with you to share and to wear and to care.

c You are smoking cigarettes again:
c I lite my lips,
c I do not spank you. I want to spank you.
c You should be spanked, ~~~~~~~~~~
~~would be a healing~~

I wish I could tell you how warm this is.
~~~~~~~~~~ this is warm.
c I want you happy, I want you warm.
c Your friend for our future, I am
Your friend in through thankfulness.
~~~~~~~~~~

[OVER]

c It is the evening of our love
~~But the Evening~~ is ripe and sweet and firm.
c Evening is fale ~~~~~~~~~~ I suffer
c Evening shall not go out,
c Evening is comforting flame
c Evening is comforting flame

Gwendolyn Brooks

Worksheets by Gwendolyn Brooks. Version 1.

FRIEND

Walking with you
shuts off shivering.
Here we are.
Here we are.

I am with you to share and to bear and to care.

This is warm.
I want you happy, I want you warm.

Your Friend for our forever is what I am.
Your Friend in thorough thankfulness.

It is the evening of our love.
Evening is hale and whole.
Evening shall not go out.
Evening is comforting flame.
Evening is comforting flame.

Worksheets by Gwendolyn Brooks. Version 2, from *Beckonings,* 1975.

The Slave Breaker
Frederick Douglass and the Slave Breaker

I could have let him lash me

       horse
like a ~~mule~~ or a dog,

to break my spirits.

         had never raised a finger
So many of us ~~had suffered passively,~~

        just one more.
I would have been ~~only one of many.~~

But something in me said, "Fight.

              for something
If it's time to die, then die fighting."
And take him along with you

So half the day we battled,

The man and the boy, sweating,

Bruising, bleeding,
~~Grunting, rolling,~~--

Till at last the slave-breaker said,

        whipped
"Go on, boy, I've ~~given~~ you enough.

Reckon now
~~You~~'ve learned your lesson."

But I knew who it was that was whipped,

   what   was.
And the lesson ~~I'd learned,~~

~~Never to forget.~~

Worksheets by Dudley Randall. Version 1.

Frederick Douglass and the Slave Breaker

I could have let him lash me
like a horse or a dog
to break my spirit.
So many of us had never raised a finger;
I would have been just one more.

But something in me said, "Fight.
If it's time to die then die for <u>some</u>thing;
and take him with you."
                    along

So half the day we battled,
the man and the boy, sweating,
bruising, bleeding,
till at last the slave-breaker said,
"Go on, boy, I done whupped you enough.
Reckon now you done learned your lesson."

But I knew who it was that was whipped,
and the lesson I learned
I'll never forget.--Dudley Randall

Worksheets by Dudley Randall. Version 2.

Frederick Douglass and The Slave Breaker

I could have let him lash me
like a horse or a dog
to break my spirit.
None of us ever lifted a finger;
I would have been just one more.

But something in me said, "Fight.
If it's time to die, then die for *something*,
and take him with you."

So all day long we battled,
the man and the boy, sweating,
bruising, bleeding . . .

till at last the slave breaker said,
"Go home, boy. I done whupped you enough.
Reckon you done learned your lesson."

But I knew who it was that was whipped,
and the lesson I learned
I'll never forget.

—DUDLEY RANDALL

Worksheets by Dudley Randall. Version 3, *Black World*, September 1972.

Frederick Douglass and the Slave Breaker

I could have let him lash me
like a horse or a dog
to break my spirit.
Others never lifted a finger.
I would have been just one more.

But something in me said, "Fight.
If it's time to die, then die for *some*thing.
And take him with you."

So all day long we battled,
the man and the boy, sweating,
bruising, bleeding . . .

till at last the slave breaker said,
"Go home, boy. I done whupped you enough.
Reckon you done learned your lesson."

But I knew who it was that was whipped.
And the lesson I learned
I'll never forget.

Worksheets by Dudley Randall. Version 4. From *After the Killing*, 1973.

P 547